Don't Stop Now!

25 Strategies to Help You Build Momentum and Keep It Going

Don't Stop Now!

A Weston Lyon & Diana Fletcher Book

Book Cover created by Melanie DePaoli
(Owner of Omicle)

ISBN: 1440419442

Our Personal Thanks to...

My parents,

Thank you for instilling in me an independent and motivated spirit!

Love, Diana

My son Haven,

Your smiling face is what keeps me going in life.

I love you with all my heart and soul!

Love, Daddy (Weston)

25 Strategies

Table of Contents

Read this FIRST!

Success in life (whatever the endeavor may be) comes down to taking action and keeping your momentum rolling forward.

That's exactly what this book is about. In <u>Don't Stop Now!</u>, you'll learn 25 strategies that Diana and I use on a regular basis to keep our momentum going.

This may sound arrogant (I assure you it's not coming from that evil place), but we know how momentum works and how to keep it moving along.

Want proof? Diana and I have published 4 books in 5 months. **Now, that's momentum!**

The strategies in this book are tried and true strategies. No theory here! So, put your seat belt on and get ready for the ride of your life.

We look forward to helping you move as fast as possible in the direction you wish to travel. Have an outstanding life and keep us posted on your progress!!!

Weston & Diana

"Cheshire Cat,' she began, rather timidly, as she did not at all know whether it would like the name: however, it only grinned a little wider.

'Come, it's pleased so far,' thought Alice, and she went on. 'Would you tell me, please, which way I ought to go from here?'

'That depends a good deal on where you want to get to,' said the Cat.

'I don't much care where'—said Alice.

'then it doesn't matter which way you go,' said the Cat.

'—so long as I get SOMEWHERE,' Alice added as an explanation.

'Oh, you're sure to do that,' said the Cat, 'if you only walk long enough.'"

Lewis Carroll
<u>Alice's Adventures in Wonderland</u>

Don't Stop Now!

Know WHY You Want Success

"Visualize your goals clearly, add desire and faith, and you will surely achieve them."

Remez Sasson

Most people set goals with their WHAT in mind – they know what they want. However, they are missing a critical component if all they know is their WHAT.

To keep your momentum going to achieve your goals you have to know **WHY** you want your goal!

It's great to know WHAT you want – you have to know that before getting anywhere. But, if you don't know WHY you want your goal, it's going to be hard to get it.

Knowing your WHY, or your reasons behind what you want, is critical.

The WHY drives you. The WHY pushes you. And the WHY keeps you going when you stumble or fall flat on your face.

You must know your WHY. You must know your reasons. And the more emotion you can put behind your reasons, the greater your chance for success.

So, don't fall for the trap of just knowing WHAT you want. Know WHY; and create a burning desire that is so strong, you can't help but achieve your goal!

Here's a simple exercise to get you started:

1. Write down WHAT you want.

2. Make a list of 5-10 reasons WHY you want that goal.

3. Read the list aloud and feel each WHY in your body. If you can't feel a build of pressure or excitement, scratch it from the list and think of another reason.

4. Continue the process until you have 5-10 reasons that make your blood boil with excitement, enthusiasm, and passion!

Don't Stop Now!

New Habits Take Time

"Habit is habit and not to be flung out of the window by any man, but coaxed downstairs a step at a time."

Mark Twain

We start something new and we are **FIRED UP!**

We have great intentions and we plan our walk. We head out there, and after we walk for half an hour, we feel good! We do it the next day and it's a little harder to get started.

The third day we think of an excuse not to go.

What happened? We know we want to get more exercise! We know we want to feel better!

"Why can't I get motivated?"

It's a matter of changing habits. I have read that it takes 21 days to change a habit. I have also read 28 days. Either way, this tells you that it doesn't happen overnight.

If you already know that it can take 21-28 days to establish the habit, tell yourself that all you have to do, is go for that amount of time.

Let's use the desire to establish a walking routine as an example for developing a new habit.

If your goal is to walk everyday, don't make this a huge

deal. Start with 10 minutes. You are trying to establish a habit, not run a marathon!

For the first week, just get yourself out that door and walk for 10 minutes! (Or get on the treadmill for ten minutes.)

If you want to walk more, fine, but remember, you want to walk everyday. You cannot store up and skip days! You are working on creating the habit.

Each day, put a big X or a gold star (fun!) on your calendar when you finish your walk.

The following week, add 5 minutes. The third week, add 5 more. At the end of 21 days, you will be walking 20 minutes a day.

And, if you can do 21 days, you can certainly do 28 days.

Continue the next week at 20 minutes.

If you are having trouble with the time, go back to 15. (Remember, you want to establish the habit—don't make this a bigger deal than it needs to be!)

Once you have done this a month, you know you can do

it! And if you can do it a month, you can do it forever!

You can do this with other activities. Break it down into shorter times, build the routine into your day, and you can establish all sorts of new habits!

Reward Yourself

"You yourself, as much as anybody in the entire universe deserves your love and affection."
Buddha

A shiny star. A treat for good behavior. A bonus in your paycheck. Ahhh...rewards.

Why don't we reward ourselves more often?

We think of it for children. We think of it for our employees. We know the concept exists.

We need to reward ourselves and we need to do this OFTEN.

Take a piece of paper and make a list of ten rewards you could give yourself. This could range from a new book to a massage. To help you make your list, ask yourself these questions:

What would feel really good after exercising everyday for a week? (Hint: a massage)

What food have I been craving, that I could let myself have once a week, and thoroughly enjoy?

What have I wanted to take the time to do? What person would I like to spend time with?

What movie would I really like to see?

I have a feeling that once you get going, you will think of new ways to reward yourself.

Life should not be about getting more done, working harder, and checking items off a to-do list. It cannot always be about your work or taking care of other people.

When you take care of yourself, you will take better care of everyone and everything else around you.

Part of taking care of you, is treating yourself to a new toy, a special outing, or time with someone you care about.

You will smile more often, you will look forward to your reward and you deserve this little addition of fun in your life!

Build Your Success Habits

"Most of the important things in the world have been accomplished by people who have kept on trying when there seemed to be no hope at all."

Dale Carnegie

Success is nothing more than doing the right things consistently. In other words, success is a series of habits strung together.

Now, while one's success cannot be duplicated exactly, because we all have different destinies, there are some habits that are universal and must be established. These habits, though tedious at times, will help you get started and keep rolling toward your success, however you define it.

A few of these habits are:

a. **Never stop learning**

Whatever endeavor you want to be successful at, you must never stop learning. The most successful people in the world are students at heart.

They are always listening to people who've succeeded before them. They can always be caught with a book in hand. They are constantly listening to audio courses and attending seminars.

Successful people study and internalize material until they know it cold.

One way to develop this habit is to make a list of people who are successful at what you desire. Then, find out what products they've created to help you do the same. Finally, buy everything they have.

I spend thousands of dollars every year on materials to get me ahead. And I'll never stop doing that because it's a habit that works. In fact, the more I make, the more I invest in myself by learning from others.

NOTE: You have to take action on this habit for it to work...there is no magic spell.

b. **Always start with your outcome in mind**

No matter what the situation, successful people know their outcome. They know it before they start. They know it while they're taking action. And they know it when they achieve it.

One way to develop this habit is by asking yourself, "What do I really want from this?"

If you keep this question in the front of your mind before doing anything, I guarantee you'll achieve better results.

It's impossible not to. When you ask a better question you automatically get a better answer. And asking what you really want is a GREAT question.

c. **Never, ever give up**

Successful people never give up, period.

They might change directions. They might pause and take a time out for a short period of time. But they never give up!

There's no really profound way of developing this habit. It's pretty much this: never, ever give up!!!

So, now that you know a few of the universal habits all successful people have developed, it's time for you to develop your own.

Use these three habits as a springboard and develop a few more of your own...you can do it, just be consistent at whatever "it" is.

Post Your Notes

"Sometimes we need a reminder that we are choosing how we spend the minutes of each day."

Diana Fletcher, Life and TotalHealth Coach

We start out with great intentions.

"I will drink more water everyday!" "I will get up and stretch every hour when I am working at my computer!"

And then, a few days later, we think, "Oh yeah...I meant to do that."

Solution: **Post it!**

There are different ways to do this. You can use the little packages of sticky paper for small areas. I actually prefer big pieces of paper with my reminders on them.

Note: This could drive the person or people you live with a little crazy. If it really bothers them, you may have to contain yourself somewhat.

I recently put up ten 8x11 squares of paper throughout my kitchen with the word **ABUNDANCE** written in large letters on each page. For some reason, although it didn't bother anyone else, this really bothered the teen-age boy. I didn't bother to explore why, and continued to concentrate on abundance. Oh well.

Our world is a very busy place. We are bombarded with calls, information, and interruptions constantly.

If we want to take an action and make a change, we need to remind ourselves of that decision, and one way to do this, is to place the reminder in our daily path.

Always forget to take your daily vitamin? Write yourself a reminder, and stick it on your cabinet where you will see it when you reach for your breakfast.

Want to remember to take bottled water with you in the car? Place a large note on the door where you exit each day.

Very Important Note: The notes and their locations do have to be changed every couple days or you will stop noticing them. They will become part of the scenery and will cease to be a reminder.

Another idea is to use different colors of paper and markers to make your reminders stand out.

This strategy can be used for all sorts of reminders.

We can use this to develop new habits and change ones

that are not serving us well anymore.

What is really fun and a great boost to our self esteem, is the moment we realize that we have successfully integrated healthy and constructive behavior into our daily lives!

Align Your Thoughts

"When you at last give your life – bringing into alignment your beliefs and the way you live, then, and only then, can you begin to find inner peace."

Peace Pilgrim

Your thoughts are the foundation of your success. Thoughts are a form of energy. Your thoughts can be categorized as either high energy or low energy.

High energy thoughts empower you, while low energy thoughts immobilize you.

In fact, as a litmus test, think of something GREAT in your life (kids, spouse, business). How does that thought make you feel? I bet you feel awesome thinking THAT thought. You may even feel like you can take on the world!

In contrast, think of something TERRIBLE in your life (finances, missed opportunities). How does that make you feel? Not so hot, huh? I bet it actually makes you feel a bit depressed or sad.

You see, your thoughts control your feelings. If you want to feel happy and successful, then think happy and successful thoughts.

Here are 3 ways to align your thoughts with the success you're after, so you can keep your momentum going:

1. Look at the people you hang around with most often.

This may not be a solution you like, but it's 100% true. The people you associate with on a regular basis, will determine your success.

Why? It's because the people you hang around on a regular basis, are the people you share most of your thoughts with, and vice versa.

Remember, thoughts are energy. And when you have friends that think with low energy, you get bombarded with that energy whether you like it or not.

Now, I'm not saying you have to abandon your friends. Not at all. Just realize you need to hang around successful people to become successful.

NOTE: The form of success is up to you. Just make sure you hang around the people who have the type of success you want.

As the immortal knight in "Indiana Jones & the Last Crusade" says, "choose, but choose wisely."

2. Think about the books you read & the CDs you listen to.

Reading and listening are two key components to becoming successful. The reason is simple...

The books you read and the CDs you listen to, enable you to think.

Now, if you're reading/listening to high-energy, thought-provoking material, you're on the right track. This kind of material will allow you think positive, high-energy thoughts.

On the other hand, if you're always reading/listening to the news, the tabloids, or whatever else that sends off bad energy, you're playing with your future.

I'm not saying you have to give this stuff up. I just want you to realize that these materials are giving off low energy and the more you read/listen to them, the more low-energy thoughts your mind produces.

Again, it's your choice, so choose wisely.

3. Pay attention to the events you attend.

By attending certain events, you can set yourself up for a lot of high-energy thoughts. Not only will you hear from great speakers that motivate, inspire, and empower you, you'll also be around a ton of people who have high energy.

This shouldn't be underestimated. The positive, high energy given off at live events is astonishing.

There are many excellent people who hold high-energy events. Here are a few:

a. Tony Robbins

If you're interested in taking control of your emotions and living a life of passion, Tony is the guy to go hear and see.

b. Dr. Wayne Dyer

If you're interested in living a peaceful, happy, spiritually-filled life, (without religious undertones), then Dr. Dyer is a must see.

c. Dan Kennedy/Bill Glazier

If you're interested in growing a business, and want to learn from the best marketers in the world, attend their events.

d. Weston Lyon/Diana Fletcher

If you're an entrepreneur and interested in having it all – family, business, and fun – you can't afford to miss our events!

Success is a matter of opinion and choice. We can be successful in many different ways. Choose the way you want success in your life and attend one of the above events – you won't regret it!!!

Retreat!

**"Adventure must start with
running away from home."**

William Bolitho

Sometimes we need to go away.

Did you ever notice how hard it can be to change habits or develop new habits, when the same old, same old, is around?

Did you ever try to think about what you want in your life and really concentrate on changes you would like to make, and you keep getting interrupted?

"I can't even finish a thought!" you find yourself saying in frustration.

If you know what I am talking about here, and you are nodding your head in agreement, then you need to go away.

A retreat can be for an hour, or it can be for a weekend.

If you have young children, it is very important to have retreats. That you love your children dearly is not the point. No one benefits from being together constantly.

You can arrange for babysitters and actually leave the house for a walk or a quiet cup of coffee somewhere. You can employ a mother's helper to play with your children, while you retreat to your bedroom and do some stretches, or lie down to rest.

You will benefit from a walk in the evening, to think, and let your thoughts drift as you walk.

A retreat can be lunch by yourself with a book, instead of going out with everyone from work, yet again, to rehash office politics.

A retreat can be a movie by yourself, or a bookstore outing.

When we let our mind be refreshed with new images and thoughts, it starts to work with possibilities, and "what ifs."

There are structured retreats and resorts that offer packages, if you can take the time. (If we try hard enough, and make it a priority, we can take the time.)

There are Hiking retreats, Yoga retreats, Spiritual Retreats. Search the internet and see what interests you.

Years ago, I did a Survival Weekend in the woods, and it was a great retreat. It was not restful, but I needed a change of scenery, and I was eager to learn new skills. That was the kind of retreat I needed at that time.

Different retreats for different times in our lives.

Do not consider yourself so indispensable that you cannot leave your life or situation for a couple days here and there.

Since my children have been very young, I take a weekend a year to go back up to Michigan to spend the time doing whatever I want. I shop with my sisters, laugh, read, visit friends, and eat when I want, whatever I want. I am not tied to anyone's schedule but my own.

This was not easy to do when the children were very young. Luckily, I have a wonderful husband who stepped into my shoes and took over.

I came back refreshed and though the relief on his face was unmistakable when I walked back through the door, we both knew it was worth it.

My husband takes a golf outing every winter. This is not always easy for him to arrange. He has to make sure everything can continue without him at work, and we have to make sure we have all bases covered at home. But, the pleasure and the relaxation he derives from his retreat, gets him through the rest of our cold, Pittsburgh winters!

We both have other trips we take, and now that the children are older, it is easier for us to arrange to be away. We try to go on trips together when the opportunity arises, or when we can create the opportunity.

You may miss your children and your partner while you are away, but remember that you need distance sometimes to realize the importance of people and situations in your life.

Being away from the same old haunts and breaking up your routine, lets you look at life from a new perspective, outside yourself and your fatigue.

A couple days of sleeping in, and changing your schedule, and you start seeing your life and your daily routines differently. You think, "Hey, why do I put up with that? Why don't I eat better? Why can't I change this? Why wouldn't this or that work...?"

It is helpful to keep some notes when you retreat.

Jotting down thoughts and feelings as you experience them instead of hoping you remember your brilliant thoughts on that hike, is a good way to bring the benefits home.

Thinking about your thoughts and feelings while you were away can help you make changes.

You may think, "How could I feel like that in my daily life?" and you come up with an idea for a breather during your work day.

You remember a great meal you had, and you think, "I could make that for myself on the weekend!"

Retreating can help you gain perspective, get new ideas, and relieve you of unrelenting work and pressure.

Try it. Go away.

Be Grateful

"Be in a continuous state of thanksgiving. You can never express thanks too often."

Alexandra Stoddard, <u>Grace Notes</u>

Those who are grateful receive more than those who aren't.

To be grateful, thankful, and appreciative, is a fundamental law of the universe that should not be ignored. And being thankful isn't hard to do. It only takes a few minutes a day to show your appreciation to your creator for everything you have. Now, I'm not talking religion here. I'm just talking about a simple conversation with your creator (whatever your beliefs).

It might be awkward at first, if you're not used to doing this, but the rewards are well worth it...astoundingly worth it!

So, whether you already feel gratitude or not, here's a simple activity to get you started in the right direction, or enhance what you're already doing:

a. Start by making a list of "life gifts" you have been given. This list may include: your family, your friends, your health, your personality, your looks, your finances, your business, your career, or whatever else you're thankful for.

b. Now, make a list of "life gifts" you wish to have. This list includes gifts that are not on your original list, but that you want in your life.

For instance, if you're not satisfied with how much money you're making right now, state the amount you would like on your second list.

Or, if you're not as fit and healthy as you'd like to be, put being fit and healthy on the second list.

Although these gifts are not in your life yet...keyword is yet...it is crucial that you become thankful for them. Once you do this, they will start appearing in your life.

c. Next, find a quiet spot. I like to walk in the woods (or somewhere alone) when I'm being grateful. It gives me the silence I need to listen, in case my source is giving me immediate answers.

d. Finally, read your lists aloud. Use your voice to feel the emotions behind each gift on your lists.

This is very important! You MUST feel your emotions.

By doing so, your brain and body will internalize what you have, want, and want more of.

Eventually, you'll be able to repeat these gifts to yourself without your notes. That's when being grateful really pays off.

The reason is simple. When you can repeat out loud what you have, want, and want more of, your brain becomes a heat seeking missile aimed at those targets.

As long as they align with your thoughts and actions, there is no end to what you can have. So, be grateful and keep that momentum going!!!

Vision Boards

"There is no use trying," Said Alice,
"One can't believe impossible things."

"I dare say you haven't had much practice," said
the Queen. "When I was your age, I always did it
for a half an hour a day. Why sometimes I have
believed as many as six impossible things before
breakfast."

Lewis Carroll, <u>Alice in Wonderland</u>

Perhaps you have heard of vision boards. Perhaps it sounds like something "way out."

And perhaps it is.

But a vision board can be a tremendous tool for you to use in defining your goals, and keeping your momentum going.

A vision board is a collection of pictures, words, and quotations that you create, to help you focus on what you want in your life.

You make a vision board yourself, because only you can decide and determine what you want and need to see on your board.

1. Supplies you will need:

Poster Board, any color, any size, or a bulletin board
Tape, glue, scissors, stapler, thumb tacks (if you are using a bulletin board), index cards
Crayons, markers, pens
Magazines
Photos
Quotes

Chances are, you already have items you can display on your vision board.

Have you ever torn out a picture from a newspaper or magazine of something that you really liked?

Have you ever copied down a quote that really struck you as interesting, wise, or funny?

Do you have favorite photos of people who you always want to keep in your life?

All of these can be included on your vision board.

2. Set up a work area for yourself.

Try to clear an hour to begin your project. You want enough time to let your mind de-clutter from everyday nonsense.

You want to take your mind to another place where you can do and have everything you want.

This is a time to let your imagination take off and soar. You are not bound by any limitations!
Allow an hour to get started, but as long as you can leave

your materials set up, you can continue your work ten minutes at a time.

3. Before you begin any of your creating, you need to take a few minutes to think.

Close your eyes. Let your imagination take off.

What would you like to be doing in the next five years?

Where would you like to travel?

What might you like to own?

Who would you like to spend time with?

What activities would you like to be involved in?

This is not the time to be sensible. This is not the time to be "realistic." Dream.

Do not let reality butt its silly head in. What if you had unlimited money? Where would you go? What would you buy? What does your ideal home look like?

4. Start with the magazines.

- Notice pictures, words and images.

- You are looking at images and thinking about individual words in a new way—what feelings do they invoke?

- What ideas do they bring to mind?

Note: Many of us have magazine subscriptions and old magazines we can use for this activity. If you don't, many libraries offer their back issues free to library patrons. You can ask friends to give you some of theirs. You can start collecting in preparation for your activity.

As you look through the magazines, do not start reading articles. (If you come across an article you would like to read, tear it out and put it aside for later.)

You can cut out words, phrases and letters to create new sentences and ideas.
Is there a word to describe a feeling, a thought, a desire?

You are putting together a board that shows you what you want in your life in the future.

This is a Dream Board, a board that points you toward your future and all that you can be and have.

As you find phrases, words, and images, start placing them on your board wherever it feels as if they should go. Do not glue, tape, or staple yet.

5. After you go through four or five magazines, stop.

Look through your photos and any quotes you have, and start to arrange those in between the other items.

6. If you know you want certain elements in your future, but there are no pictures to describe these, pick up your crayons or markers, and write the words on an index card.

Perhaps there is a city or country you dream of seeing. If you can't find a picture of it, write the place name in large letters and include it. There are no practicalities allowed here! Dream!

Perhaps you have always wanted to go back to school to earn a degree, or to take some fun classes.

Don't stop yourself with practical limitations or reasons why you can't do something. This isn't the place for limited thinking.

7. Place the words, My Vision, at the top of your board. You can write this yourself, or cut out the letters from your magazines.

8. Arrange your vision pieces on your board.

Move pictures around and arrange your words, quotes, etc.

9. It is time to tape, staple, or use your push pins for your bulletin board.

Step back admire the results of your effort.

10. Hang your Vision Board in a place where you will notice it often.

This is going to be a reminder everyday that you are in

charge of your destiny and your life.

This is a reminder that you have permission to dream.

This is a freedom ticket—you are allowed to go wherever you want in your imagination. It allows you to think beyond the limitations of money and responsibilities and "real life."

This is your vision and each day, you need to spend a few minutes looking at it. Really looking at it and thinking about it.

And this is what you may find happens...

Everyday, you see the places you want to go, and suddenly one day, you think of an idea that will help you to save the money to make that trip a reality.

You look at it everyday, and suddenly you realize that going back to school is not such a silly idea, and it is possible.

We limit ourselves more often than any circumstance ever could.

Vision Boards are about DREAMING and about MAKING DREAMS COME TRUE.

Change Your Attitude
by Tricking Your Brain

" ...Attitude keeps me going or cripples my progress. It alone fuels my fire or assaults my hope.
When my attitudes are right, there is no barrier
too high, no valley too deep, no dream too ex-
treme, no challenge too great for me."

Charles R. Swindoll

Sometimes it is so hard to get fired up to do what we know we really want to do. We get tired, life makes us weary, and we feel frustrated.

So, it's time to trick yourself. You must tell yourself thoughts that you may not even believe.

You must put pictures into your mind to trick your brain and change your attitude.

Let me explain.

It can be really hard to stay on your chosen path some-times. You work hard and you feel as if you are making no progress.

You reach a plateau in your weight loss struggles, you feel stuck, or the novelty of the new exercise program has worn off.

You are trying to stay the course with some work issues, and you aren't seeing the results yet anywhere that you look.

It's time to lie to your brain.

Let me tell you how I used this trick this past year. I

have a teen-age boy, and for those of you who have teen-agers, that is probably all I need to say. For those who don't, let me explain.

Teen-agers, and especially boys, go temporarily insane for awhile. You do not recognize this person as the same child you raised.

This period of insanity could last anywhere from a year to a few years. It is a very frustrating time for parent and child, and it can be very difficult to remember that you love this person, and really difficult to remember that sometimes you even liked this person.

So your attitude becomes one of wacko-parent and you find yourself saying and doing things you never expected to say or do.

Enter, attitude change.

I went through my photo album, and picked out pictures of my son with me, with my husband, and by himself. All the pictures were of happy times.

I took some of the pictures and put them on the visor in my van so I would see them when I pulled it down. One picture, in which he looked especially cute, I put on my bedroom dresser. I distributed these pictures throughout my world—my office, the kitchen, the laundry room, and in my organizer.

Throughout my day, I would be reminded of how much I cared about him, and many times I found myself smiling at the picture.

I still got frustrated, but something about my attitude changed. I became more patient, and in turn, he seemed more reasonable.

He is a great kid and we have survived, but I know this "tricking of the brain" was what I needed to do. My brain needed to remember and tell me that I loved him still.

You can use this idea in many ways.

Write out statements describing the result you want, as if you already have it. Put this in front of you and read it over and over during the day.

Use my idea of a photograph or make a drawing to make you think in a different way. It doesn't matter if you believe this stuff right away—it matters that you keep showing and telling your brain something different than the negative messages it has been receiving.

Perhaps you can post a picture of clothing you are going to be able to wear when you reach your weight loss goal.

Act as if a situation is going exactly how you want it to go. Think of your goals as already achieved, and let yourself feel the happy emotions that accompany that success.

Write out a statement telling yourself how happy you are with the results. Look at this statement everyday.

Your brain will start feeling the emotions, and your experiences may begin to feel different to you.

Let your brain start working for you, instead of against you. What a powerful comrade to have on your side!

Meditate

"Meditation can recharge our mental batteries,
make us feel more alert, and provide us with
calm resolve. This gives us the capacity to handle
different situations rather than get caught up
in reactivity."

Christopher Titmuss, <u>The Power of Meditation</u>

Some of you may think I've gone completely off my rocker here. After all, how can sitting down trying to be at peace with the world, (most people's definition of meditation), continue to move you toward your goals and dreams?

I asked the exact same question years ago. And you know what I found out? Nothing!

Because I did nothing. I didn't believe meditation could help me create and sustain momentum in my life so I never tried it.

As Julia Roberts, in Pretty Woman, said to the salesgirl who didn't service her, "Big mistake. BIG, HUGE!"

You see, it's only been in the past 12 months that I've started meditating on a daily basis. And in that time frame, my business has doubled and my productivity has quintupled.

Has it all been from meditation? Maybe not.

BUT, one, why mess with a good thing? And two, meditation has brought me to a place in my life where my work just flows.

Things get done quickly and with less effort. Projects materialize in days or weeks instead of months or years. Life is all around just easier.

That's what I want for you. So, here's a meditation to get you started down the path of being more productive, of making more money, of living an easier life, and whatever else you want:

a. Sit down in a quiet place and turn off ALL phones, cell phones, crackberries, or anything else that goes buzz, beep, or sings songs.

b. Take 5 deep breaths from your diaphragm. This will help you clear your mind.

c. Now, as you continue to breathe deeply, let your mind wander.

Don't think of anything in particular...just let go and allow thoughts to flow in and out of your mind without trying to grab any of them.

If you catch a thought by accident and start focusing on it, relax and just let it go.

d. Congratulations! You just meditated. Nothing to it, huh?

Okay, so what makes this so special?

One, you're learning to relax. And in today's fast-paced, all-go-no-stop world, you need to relax.

Two, you're teaching your mind to stir up creative juices when you're relaxed. The more creative juices are flowing, the more you can get done in a shorter period of time. (Most people take time to think about what they want to do instead of just letting it flow.)

And three...you're not just meditating to meditate. By practicing meditation, you will receive answers to questions that have been eluding you for hours, days, and even weeks.

You see, your subconscious mind works better when you're relaxed and NOT thinking. Let your subconscious mind do its thing and you'll reap the benefits with huge amounts of momentum!

Create a Plan

"Reduce your plan to writing. The moment
you complete this, you will have definitely given
concrete form to the intangible desire."

Napoleon Hill

Make a simple plan.

Most people fail because they make their plan too elaborate.

I'm not saying complex plans are bad – they're not. It's what you do with these plans that determine if the complexity is good or bad.

Most people who make a plan create an elaborate scheme on multiple pages. They write everything down!

Now, it's good to have a "master plan." But if you want to keep your momentum going and achieve your goals, it's best to make your plans as simple as possible.

Here's what to do:

1. Write out your elaborate scheme. Write down everything that comes to mind and how you plan on achieving each step.

2. Zero in on the important things to keep in front of you and put them all on ONE page.

3. Now you have a reference guide to look at to make sure you're doing what needs to be done. This one page is your core plan.

4. Keep your "master plan," but keep your core plan in front of you at all times. Read it every day for best results.

Don't Stop Now!

Momentum for the Long Haul

"Nothing could be worse than the fear that one had given up too soon, and left one unexpended effort that might have saved the world."

Jane Addams

What if you are trying to keep up your momentum for something that is going to take a long time?

Perhaps you are starting a new position as a supervisor of an office. You know it will take awhile to implement your plans, establish new procedures, and gain the respect of your employees.

What if you are launching a program, and a large part of accomplishing this depends on other people coming through for you? You are not controlling everything.

What if you are determined to finish a degree, but you are getting tired and it still seems so far away?

There are a couple techniques you can use here.

One, it's important to look at the big picture. Remind yourself of what you want in the long run.

It may be helpful to make a list of all the great things that will come about when you reach your goal. (More money, a degree, a promotion, a new product)

Two, make a list of what will happen if you don't reach your goal. (You'll still reach the same age---the time will pass anyway, you'll feel bad.)

Keep both these lists where you can see and read them everyday.

Three, when your goals depend on other people, make sure you are keeping up your end of things. Have your work done on time, and suggest weekly progress report meetings.

Some people need the reminders, or their partner and group projects get forgotten. Work together on deadlines to keep everyone accountable.

Four, be patient. When you are working to change the way things are done in a new office or you are re-working your own strategies, be patient.

⋇ Break tasks down into smaller parts.

⋇ Make a realistic timeline for yourself and chart your progress. Sometimes we get frustrated with how slowly things seem to be moving, but if we look back, we realize a lot has been accomplished.

⋇ Reward yourself and your employees. Make sure you pat yourself and others on the back for steps taken toward your goals.

Don't Stop Now!

It can be frustrating when you need to keep going and aren't exactly sure when the end will come. But it will, and the benefits you will achieve from sticking with something, are incredible.

You will see what you're capable of, and it will inspire you to bigger and better endeavors. You will be more inspired than ever, and you will be an inspiration to others!

Track Your Progress
(Method 1)

**"An intelligent plan is the first step to success.
The man who plans knows where he is going,
knows what progress he is making and has a
pretty good idea when he will arrive."**

Basil S. Walsh

To make any change you have to become aware. More specifically, you have to become aware of what IS working and what IS NOT working.

You see, most people who do track their progress, just take a look at where they are and where they're going. That's important, but they don't look at what is and is not working.

This is a big faux pas.

If something IS working, do more of it! If something IS NOT working, either stop doing it, or keep that in mind as you test it.

Either way, you MUST know what is, and what is not working. This information is crucial if you want to build momentum and achieve your goal.

Here's a simple exercise to help you track your progress:

1. At the end of each week, sit down and write out what you did that week.

2. Next to each item you finished, comment if it worked or did not work.

3. If it worked, write that down on a separate sheet of paper. At the top of that sheet write SUCCESSES. If it didn't work, write that on another sheet of paper. Mark that sheet as TESTS.

4. After you have all your successes on one page, write down why you think it worked, and how you can implement it even more.

5. On the "TESTS" page, write down why you think it failed and how you could do it better so it does succeed.

6. If one of your TESTS isn't right for your goal, toss it and move on.

Now, you have a list of what works, what doesn't, and what you can test again. Keep tracking your progress and testing. Momentum and success aren't far off!

Don't Stop Now!

Track Your Progress
(Method II)

**"Be Not Afraid of going slowly,
be only afraid of standing still."**

Chinese Proverb

Another way to track your progress is to actually chart it.

When I was training for a marathon a couple years ago, I made a chart for the seven months I would be training.

I was using a book by Jeff Galloway to help me train, and he had 6-month schedules for different goals. I was using the "I just want to finish," training schedule. (Really.)

I adapted his scheduling for the 7 months I had until the March 26th marathon. I knew each day what I had to do to prepare for my run. On the alternate days, I chose which exercise I would do, and I wrote that down. I did not want to neglect my strength training, or lose track of what week, and what distance, I was supposed to be do-ing.

I posted my homemade schedule/chart on the fridge.

I got so much pleasure out of seeing my progress, day by day, and week by week, and finally month by month! I drew a line through each day as I completed the activity, and the more I did, the more I wanted to draw those lines each day!

A chart can be used to track exercise progress. It can be as detailed as my marathon training chart, or as simple as a month-long calendar where you record how much you walk each day, and record totals at the end of the week. (It is fun to add up the times and miles later and pat yourself on the back!)

You can chart how much water you are drinking, or how many days you resist that chocolate that is sitting on someone's desk at work. You can record how many days you managed to read a few pages of your book.

A chart enables you to actually see your goals in writing and gives you an accurate take on your progress.
You can keep your chart private or post it on the fridge as I did. Whatever works for you.

This is not a technique for everyone but it is worth trying for even a few days. It could be just the thing to keep up your momentum!

Don't Stop Now!

Create a Dream List

**"I don't dream at night, I dream all day;
I dream for a living."**

Steven Spielberg

This may sound a bit whoo-hoo, or alien to you, but I assure you, this tactic works.

I created my first dream list when I was in my early 20's. I was listening to a speaker on tape, (an actual cassette because I couldn't afford a CD player in my car) talk about how he built his business from a small, just-getting-by-business, to a massive empire in 12 short months.

On the tape, he revealed his secret to doing this...you got it, creating a dream list.

When I first heard this, I thought he was insane. But having nothing to lose I wrote my first dream list when I got home that night.

It isn't as easy as it sounds, which you'll find out soon enough. In fact, it's a damn struggle. But that's what makes it so valuable. We'll get to that in a moment...

Anywho, after creating my first dream list, nothing magically happened – at least not at first. However, after a few short months, things on my list starting coming true.

Was it magic? Of course not.

So, what was it? First, allow me to show you how you can create your own dream list and then I'll tell you why I think it worked for me and why I think it will work for you:

1. Sit down in a quiet area with no distractions. Grab a plain white notepad and a blue pen.

2. Now, on the top of your first page, write in BIG BOLD letters: 101 Dreams

3. Next, start listing your dreams on the left hand side. When you hit the bottom, create a second column on the right side of the page and continue writing. Write whatever comes to mind. Whatever you want to do, be, or have...**WRITE IT DOWN!**

4. When you get to about 60 or so, you'll understand what I meant before when I said this can be a struggle. Don't stop. Keep thinking of stuff you want and write it ALL down.

Okay, now that you have your list let me give you a few last instructions and tell you why this works (my opinion at least).

a. Make sure you read this list everyday.

b. When you accomplish one of your dreams on the list, highlight it and write VICTORY beside it (preferably in lavender-- a trick a learned a while later from Mark Victor Hansen).

c. Never throw this away. I made this mistake, and I wish I could go back and re-visit my past dreams and accomplishments.

So, why does this work? In my humble opinion, I think there are 3 reasons:

1. Clarity

Having 101 dreams on a sheet of paper really brings your life into prospective. You know have no excuse to be lazy because you know exactly what you want.

2. Focus

When you finally have what you really want on paper, you can focus instead of just wishing. Life is too short to wish...you have to **act** if you want to dream bigger.

3. Purpose

Dexter Yager says, "When the dream's big enough, the facts don't count."

And the facts don't count if you get passionate about your dream list. Write your list and pile on that momentum like no one's business.

Don't Stop Now!

Entice Yourself

"How much time, creative energy, and emotion
do we expend resisting change because we
assume growth must always be painful?"

Sarah Ban Breathnach, <u>Simple Abundance</u>

According to the dictionary, to entice means to attract by offering hope of reward or pleasure. Entice yourself.

Here are the ways you can do this:

1. Rent a really good movie. Insert it into the DVD player in front of your treadmill. Only allow yourself to watch the movie when you are on the treadmill. This will get you there for three or four days in a row. Then, get another movie!

2. If you want to get up earlier in the morning, pick out some really good coffee and set the coffee maker to start brewing 10 minutes before your alarm clock goes off. Let the aroma pull you out of that comfortable bed. Not a coffee drinker? Buy some of the wonderful teas that are out there and place the tea leaves next to your bed to remind you of what's waiting for you.

3. Do you like a good story? Get some books on CDs, and the next time you have a long drive that you are dreading, pop those CDs in and let the miles fly by.

4. Make your work area welcoming. Make sure your chair supports you and is comfortable. Clear the area of clutter. Make sure you like the way things feel and look.

Let yourself be pulled to an attractive place to get things done. Make your work area a nice place to be with artwork, plants or candles. Think of what will lure you into the area.

Take a little time and think. I am sure you can come up with something to entice yourself.

Don't Stop Now!

Create a Mastermind

"...when a group of individual brains is coordinated and functions in harmony, the increased energy created through that alliance becomes available to every individual brain in the group."

Napoleon Hill, <u>Think and Grow Rich</u>

A mastermind is a group of like-minded people who are trying to achieve more. Here are 3 reasons you might consider creating your own mastermind group:

1. **Accountability** – Like a coach, a mastermind group will keep you accountable to someone other than yourself.

Being accountable is far superior.

2. **Competition** – A mastermind can spark some friendly competition. It's natural to feel a sense of competitiveness when you hear and see others succeeding.

That competitiveness will either push you to compete with them or with yourself...either way, you'll feel compelled to move forward faster.

3. **Conditioning** – A mastermind group allows you to condition yourself for success. When you think about it, success is nothing more than doing the right things over and over again.

When you're in a mastermind, you get the opportunity to share your successes to help the other people. It just so happens though, when you teach, you learn twice.

In other words, when you help others by giving them ex-amples of yourself, you condition your brain with the suc-cesses you're discussing. The more you talk about your successes, the more you will continue those activities, and the more you will succeed.

Sounds good, eh? Well, here are 4 steps to help you start your own mastermind – a group that will help you keep your momentum running strong:

1. Pick a date and time, and create a structure for your mastermind group.

An easy structure for beginners is: have each member talk about their successes over the past week or month, have each member comment on the other members' "talk," and wrap up with actions each member will ac-complish before the next meeting.

2. Write a list of 5 people you know (or want to learn from) who are high achievers.

3. Call each one and tell them you're forming a master-mind group and you thought of them. Tell them what will be involved (structure, date, time), and ask them to join.

4. If someone declines (which will happen), choose someone else and move on. Just make sure you have 5-8 people so the meetings are productive.

Mastermind groups can meet in person or over the phone. They can meet weekly, or once a month. You may want to give the mastermind a 6 month try-out, to see if everyone works well together.

Your group may inspire and take you to successes you couldn't have dreamed of by yourself.

Diana Fletcher & Weston Lyon

Don't Stop Now!

Keep a Journal

"Journal writing is a voyage to the interior."

Christina Baldwin

Writing in a journal can be helpful for some people as a way to keep momentum going.

It is important to write each day as a way of viewing what is going on in your life, and what progress you are making.

I write in a journal each morning, though this does require an earlier wake-up time before anyone else gets up. I find that I need the quiet of the morning.

I write about the previous day and all the things I did and thought about.

I look ahead and plan what I will do with the day ahead. I like to keep a legal pad next to my journal and write out lists of phone calls, errands and other activities I need to do that day.

As I write, I am reviewing what I have done, what I have accomplished and my thoughts and feelings about those items.

No one else ever sees my journals, so I am able to be completely honest.

I may notice that I am repeating myself and that tells me

to get cracking on certain tasks.

I notice that I write about an emotional issue and realize it is something to resolve.

I think about friends as I write, and it reminds me to call them or write to them.

It is a check-in with myself, and I encourage people to do this.

If you have never done journal writing before, here is how you can get started:

1. Buy a notebook or journal. There are journals everywhere and you may like to look at all the different designs and types. Pick one that appeals to you.

2. Pick out a pen that writes smoothly and fits in your hand comfortably.

3. Decide on a time to write. For many people, evening is a good time to go over the day, and to plan ahead for the next day.

For some, morning will work best. Try to allow 15 minutes or more to write.

4. If you are unsure how to start, just write about that. ("I don't know what to write, but here I am...")

5. Do this for a week, then decide if journal writing is for you.

Involve a Partner

"Two friends, two bodies, with one soul inspired."

Homer

Let's face it. Many times, the only reason you showed up for the event, the walk, or the family gathering is that you had promised someone that you would.

You wake up and think "I so do not want to do <u>fill in the blank</u> today!"

Then you remember that you told your neighbor, your best friend, or your co-worker, that you would be there for sure! So, you go.

Use that same idea to get the results you want in your life.

For example, if you want to make sure you walk, find someone else who wants to walk. Make a commitment to each other to meet at a certain time and day, no matter what.

Besides the fact that you will stick to your plan more often, this also can make the activity more fun.

If you really want to stick with a plan, find someone you trust, and ask them if you can report to them weekly. You can tell them of your progress on a book you are writing, a topic you are studying, or the product you are creating.

Their encouragement can do wonders for your self-esteem and help you stick to deadlines.

Just a warning: It is easier to involve a partner who does not live with you. It is too tempting for us to take reminders from a spouse, roommate, or partner, as nagging, and it makes it hard for that person to continue being in that role.

If you do not have someone to attend an exercise class with, meet for walks, or have weekly progress report sessions, this is the time when hiring a coach could work for you.

Don't Stop Now!

Find a Coach

"A coach can help you clarify your goals, decide on
what action steps you want and need, and will
cheer you on, all the way. A coach provides an
incredible support and accountability system."

Diana Fletcher, Life and TotalHealth Coach

Finding a coach is essential to your success...at least, if you want a high level of success.

Hey, Michael Jordan had a coach. Tiger Woods has a coach. And you need a coach. But not just any coach...a coach that fits your needs.

So, here are a few things to look for in a coach to fit your needs:

a. A coach who's achieved what you want

We've been over-populated with coaches in the past few years in every area of life.

Now, that's not a bad thing, but coaches aren't all the same. When you choose your coach, make sure they have achieved what you're looking to accomplish.

So, if you're looking to lose weight, find a coach who looks how you want to look.

If you're looking to get a big project done (like write a book), find a coach who's written a book.

It sounds simple, but it's overlooked way too often.

b. A coach who cares about you as a person.

I don't mean a coach who cares just about your progress with them. I mean someone who cares about YOU.

Listen, while results are the reason you came to your coach at first, caring about you as a person is more important.

Why? Because people make mistakes. People procrastinate...even with a coach. You want someone who cares about you and what's going on with you, personally.

If you find a coach like that, keep 'em. You'll eventually get the results you crave. It just so happens there may be something holding you back that a "progress-only" coach can't see. But a "person-caring" coach can.

NOTE: This is a two way street. Make sure you're giving back good energy and listening. If you don't, your coach may be too drained to help you.

c. A coach who coaches

I know this sounds redundant, but hear me out.

A coach who spits information at you is NOT a coach. They're a teacher or a trainer.

A real coach is someone who listens to where you are – mentally, emotionally, physically, and spiritually – and gives you sound advice on how to get to where you want to go, while maneuvering you through your self-inflicted barriers.

So choose, but choose wisely. The right coach will help you get you to your goal, while the wrong coach will take your money (without caring about you) and waste your energy.

Renew Your Commitment

"I believe life is constantly testing us for our level
of commitment, and life's greatest rewards are re-
served for those who demonstrate a never-ending
commitment to act until they achieve. This level
of resolve can move mountains, but it must be
constant and consistent. As simplistic as this
may sound, it is still the common denominator
separating those who live their dreams from
those who live in regret."

Anthony Robbins

Making a commitment is a one-time occurrence, right?

WRONG!

That's the trap. Most people make their commitment a one-time occurrence. While the ideal would be that we would only have to make a commitment once, it doesn't work. We're human! We make mistakes. We slip up.

That's why your commitment needs to be reviewed and renewed EVERYDAY! I know that seems like a lot of work, but it's vital to your success.

How many times have you "committed" yourself to a goal and not achieved it? If you're like me, it's happened more times than you'd like to admit.

How many times have you said, "I'm going to get this done," only to wake up 6 months down the road, and re-alize you're not one step closer?

It's happened to all of us. The trick to avoid this trap is to review and renew your commitments everyday.

Commit everyday and nothing can stop you!

Walking

"Walking is Meditation in Motion."

Weston Lyon

Walking may seem like a funny activity to include in a book about keeping up your momentum. But it is amazing what walking can do.

It is not just exercise. Walking is a wonderful way to clear your head of the clutter, and mentally re-frame.

When you are stuck on a problem, a walk can bring you the answers. You leave your office, your desk, your home, and you walk.

You don't necessarily concentrate on your problem as you walk. In fact, I advise not trying to work out the solution. Let your mind drift as your feet move.

Take in the fresh air and let your eyes take in the sights, your ears the sounds.

Even a ten minute walk can refresh you and give you new insight into a solution that you thought would never come.

A walk every day will do far more for you than any amount of concentrating and staring at a project could ever do. It becomes a break in your day, a reward to look forward to.

It becomes your time to welcome new thoughts and ideas. It refreshes your body and spirit, and it can keep your momentum going in the right direction.

Don't Stop Now!

Do Something Fun – Everyday!

**"...we take ourselves and our lives
too seriously sometimes. Lighten up."**

Weston Lyon, <u>Fun Re-defined</u>

Don't Stop Now!

Life's too short, so have fun!

Seriously. Doing something fun or silly, or even goofy, everyday, is a necessity if you want to keep your momentum going.

Being silly and having fun will help rejuvenate your mind and body. It will make you feel alive. And it will shoot energy and enthusiasm through your veins!

Our book, <u>Fun Re-defined</u>, offers 33 strategies to have fun with, but here's one to get you started:

Sing to Yourself

1. Grab some music that makes you feel good inside.

2. Now, pull down the shades in your home...no voyeurs allowed.

3. Turn the music on full blast (without going deaf) and sing, sing, sing!!!

You're alone, so belt it out. Don't be shy. Just sing to have fun.

Hey, and while you're at it, dance along with the music. It doesn't matter what you dance like...you're alone. So, have a blast and enjoy yourself.

This might sound immature, but you need to relax and let go. The more fun you have in your life, the easier it will be for you to sustain your momentum.

Whatever you decide to do... have fun everyday!

Don't Stop Now!

Notice How Good It Feels

"I can't change the direction of the wind, but I can adjust my sails to always reach my destination."

Jimmy Dean

Now that you've created and sustained your momentum toward success, (your success), it's time to notice how good you feel.

A lot of successful people are in achievement overdrive. They achieve and achieve, and then achieve some more. They never slow down to "smell the roses." They never stop and enjoy themselves.

The problem with this is: **they eventually burn out.**

They don't understand the success cycle every over-achiever (who continues to achieve every year) uses:

1. **Create a burning desire.**
2. **Take action.**
3. **Achieve!**
4. **Relax and Ponder.**
5. **Repeat cycle.**

People who burn out, have missed step #4. They don't relax and they don't ponder. This is muy importante!

Relaxing, pondering, and becoming aware of your success and how it makes you feel is critical to your future success. It's NOT a step to miss.

Here are 3 emotions to ponder after you succeed (to keep your momentum!)

1. Happiness

It's important to be happy. So ponder this:

Are you happy with what you're moving toward?
Are you happy with the decisions you've made so far on your journey?
Are you happy? Just happy?

2. Calmness

The older I get, the more I realize how important it is to stay calm when I'm in achievement mode. It's taken me a while to understand this...here's something to ponder:

Achievement in life is like water. Push it and it will move away from you. Pull it and it will move around you. Grasp it and it will slip through your fingers. The harder you try, the more it eludes you.

So, what does all this mean? I'm not telling you. I know what it means to me. But it will be different for you.

Ponder this statement and see what you come up with.

A hint: Don't try too hard. If you do, the answer will slip through your fingers.

3. Righteousness

You're allowed to change your mind. If you're headed in a direction that doesn't feel right, change directions.

Ponder this:

Do you feel like you're moving in the right direction?

Do you feel good about your decisions...are they right for you?

What could you do to make your decisions and actions feel even better?

Become aware of your feelings and notice how good it feels. You're on your way...keep your momentum going!

The End...

Now that you've finished reading <u>Don't Stop Now!</u>, it's time to go back and circle, highlight, or dog-ear the strategies you want to take action with.

As you can see, building momentum isn't hard, but it does take work. Take all of these strategies and create the momentum you need to excel in life.

You know what you want. You've created space to succeed. You're taking action toward your dreams. Don't Stop Now...keep the momentum going!

We look forward to hearing from you and/or seeing you at an upcoming event. We wish you all the best on your journey.

Have an Outstanding Life!

Weston & Diana

Don't Stop Now!

Weston Lyon & Diana Fletcher are the nation's lead-ing experts on helping crazy-busy entrepreneurs have it all - *family, business, and fun!*

Together they have written 4 books:

Creating Space

Fun Re-defined

Don't Stop Now!

7 Steps to Start Living an Outstanding Life

All 4 books are part of the <u>Outstanding Life Series</u> and can be found at:

<u>www.CreatingAnOutstandingLife.com</u>

Claim Your FREE Gifts NOW!

($319 Value)

FREE E-Book

"7 Strategies to Create Time in Your Crazy-Busy Life"
E-book (a $16 value)

FREE Tele-seminar

"7 Strategies to Create Time in Your Crazy-Busy Life"
Tele-seminar (a $79 value)

FREE Special Report

"Mastering the 3 Patterns that Control Your Life"
Confidential Special Report (a $27 value)

FREE Subscription

To our internationally recognized weekly e-zine for
crazy-busy entrepreneurs, Have It All! (a $197 value)

Claim your gifts right now... *FREE!*

www.CreatingAnOutstandingLife.com

 ## Books in Print by Diana Fletcher & Weston Lyon

Creating Space - $17.00

Fun Re-defined - $14.95

Don't Stop Now! - $15.95

7 Steps to Start Living an Outstanding Life- $49.97

All available at
www.CreatingAnOutstandingLife.com

*****

The Fastest Workout Ever!
$49.97
Available at **www.TheFastestWorkoutEver.com**

The Common Sense Golfer
$24.95
Available at **www.CommonSenseGolfer**

Time Mastery Secrets for Entrepreneurs
$12.95
Available at
www.BookOfSecretsForEntrepreneurs.com

The End

...Now Get to Work!!!

www.ingramcontent.com/pod-product-compliance
Lightning Source LLC
Chambersburg PA
CBHW051540170526
45165CB00002B/815